RED TAYLOR SWIFT

UKULELE

ISBN 978-1-4803-2164-9

HAL•LEONARD® CORPORATION

7777 W. BLUEMOUND RD. P.O. BOX 13819 MILWAUKEE, WI 53213

Visit Hal Leonard Online at
www.halleonard.com

CONTENTS

4 STATE OF GRACE

16 RED

22 TREACHEROUS

26 I KNEW YOU WERE TROUBLE

9 ALL TOO WELL

30 22

34 I ALMOST DO

40 WE ARE NEVER EVER GETTING BACK TOGETHER

45 STAY STAY STAY

50 THE LAST TIME

64 HOLY GROUND

68 SAD BEAUTIFUL TRAGIC

74 THE LUCKY ONE

57 EVERYTHING HAS CHANGED

78 STARLIGHT

83 BEGIN AGAIN

State of Grace

Words and Music by Taylor Swift

Chorus

And I nev - er _____ saw you ___ com - ing. _____

And I'll nev - er _____ be the ___ same. _____

To Coda 2 ⊕   *D.C. al Coda 1*

⊕ **Coda 1**

four blue ___ eyes. ___

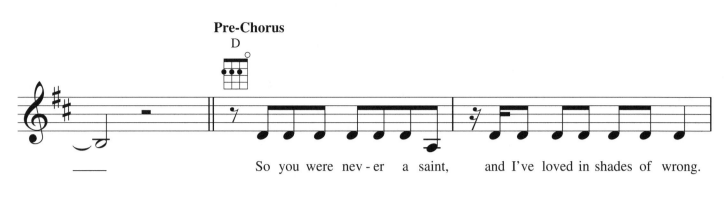

Pre-Chorus

So you were nev-er a saint, and I've loved in shades of wrong.

We learn to live with the pain, mo-sa-ic bro-ken hearts. But this love is

D.S. al Coda 2

brave and _____ wild. _____ And I

Coda 2

Bridge

This is a state of grace. This is the worth-while __

_____ fight. Love is a ruth-less game _____ un-less __

_____ you play __ it good and __ right. These are the hands __ of

fate. _____ You're my A - chil - les' heel. _____

This is the gold - en age _____ of some - thing good _____ and right ___ and ___

_____ real. And I nev - er _____

Chorus

_____ saw you ___ com - ing. _____

And I'll nev - er _____

be the ___ same. ___

I

This is a state of grace. This is the worth - while ___

___ fight. Love is a ruth - less game ___ un - less ___

___ you play ___ it good and ___ right. ___

All Too Well

Words and Music by Taylor Swift and Liz Rose

Verse

sweet dis - po - si - tion and my wide - eyed __ gaze, __ we're

(3.) *See additional lyrics*

sing - in' in the car, __ get - tin' lost __ up - state. __

Au - tumn leaves __ fall - in' down like piec - es in - to place, __ and I _____

_____ can pic - ture it af - ter all _____ these days. __ And I

Pre-Chorus

know it's long __ gone __ and that mag - ic's not __ here __ no more, and I

might be o - kay, __ but I'm not fine at all. _____

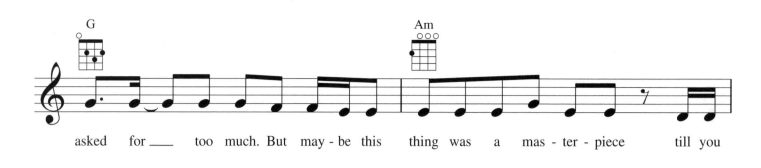

asked for ___ too much. But may-be this thing was a mas-ter-piece till you

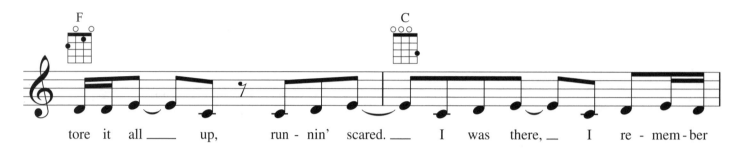

tore it all ___ up, run-nin' scared. ___ I was there, ___ I re-mem-ber

it all ___ too ___ well. ___ And you

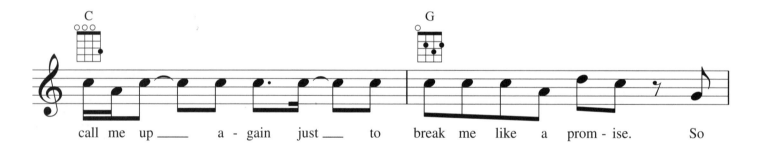

call me up ___ a-gain just ___ to break me like a prom-ise. So

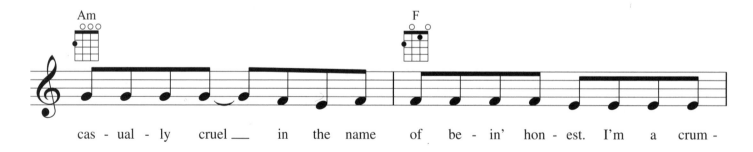

cas-ual-ly cruel ___ in the name of be-in' hon-est. I'm a crum-

pled-up piece of pa-per ly-in' here, 'cause I re-mem-ber it ___ all, ___

_____ all, _____ all _____ too well. __

Verse

4. Time won't __ fly; ___ it's like I'm par - a - lyzed by it. I'd like to

be my old self ___ a - gain, but I'm still tryin' to find ___ it af - ter

plaid shirt __ days __ and nights when you made me your own. _____ Now you

mail back my things __ and I walk home a - lone. __ But you

Chorus

14

Outro

it all ___ too ___ well. ___

___ Wind in my hair, ___ you were there, ___ you re - mem - ber

it all. ___ Down the stairs, ___ you were there, ___ 'cause you re -

mem - ber it all. ___ It was rare, ___ I was there, ___ I re - mem - ber

it all ___ too ___ well. ___

Additional Lyrics

3. Photo album on the counter, your cheeks were turnin' red.
   You used to be a little kid with glasses in a twin-size bed.
   Your mother's tellin' stories 'bout you on the tee-ball team.
   You tell me 'bout your past, thinkin' your future was me.

Pre-Chorus: And I know it's long gone and there was nothin' else I could do.
   And I forget about you long enough to forget why I needed to.

Chorus: 'Cause there we are again in the middle of the night.
   We're dancin' 'round the kitchen in the refrigerator light.
   Down the stairs, I was there, I remember it all too well.

Red

Words and Music by Taylor Swift

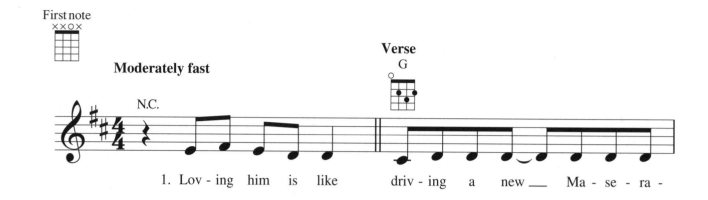

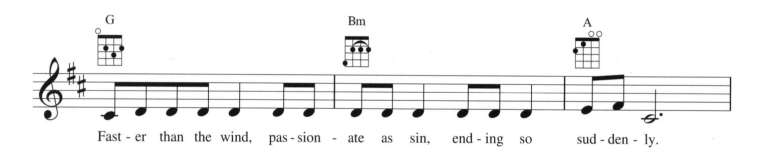

1. Lov - ing him is like driv - ing a new __ Ma - se - ra - ti down a dead - end street. __

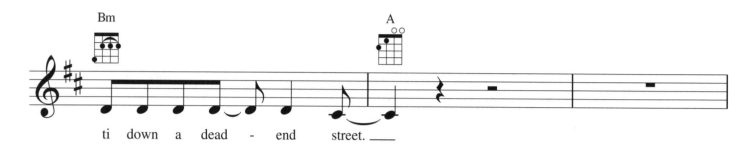

Fast - er than the wind, pas - sion - ate as sin, end - ing so sud - den - ly.

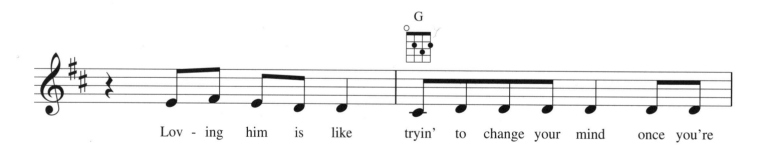

Lov - ing him is like tryin' to change your mind once you're

al - read - y flyin' __ through the free __ fall, like the

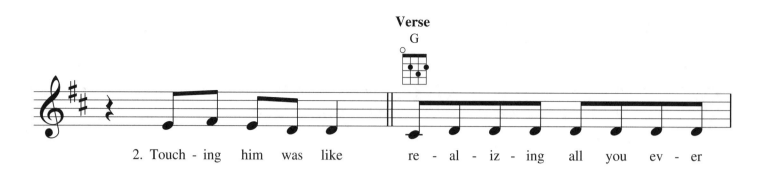

Verse

2. Touch - ing him was like re - al - iz - ing all you ev - er

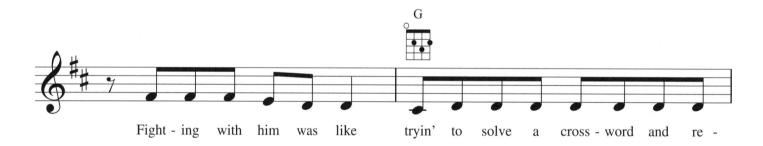

want - ed was right __ there in front of you. Mem - o - riz - ing him was as

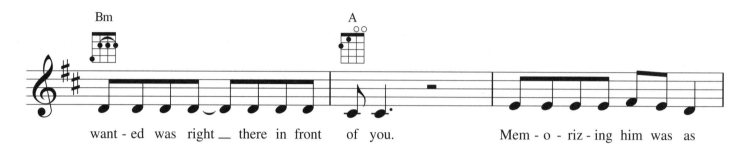

eas - y as know - ing all the words __ to your old __ fa - v'rite song.

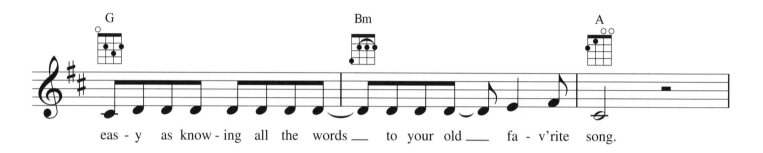

Fight - ing with him was like tryin' to solve a cross - word and re -

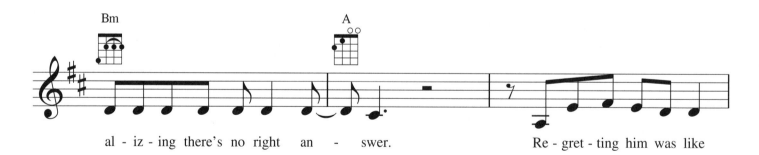

al - iz - ing there's no right an - swer. Re - gret - ting him was like

wish - ing you nev - er found out _____ that love could be that _____ strong. __

Treacherous

Words and Music by Taylor Swift and Dan Wilson

First note

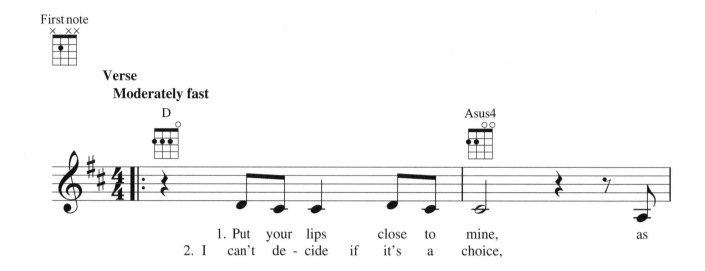

Verse
Moderately fast

1. Put your lips close to mine, as
2. I can't de - cide if it's a choice,

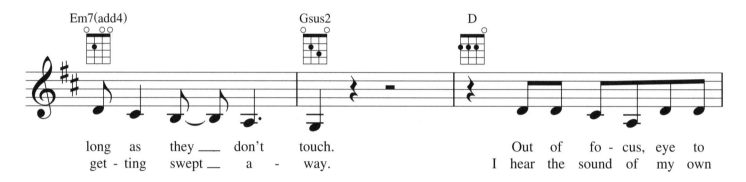

long as they __ don't touch.
get - ting swept __ a - way.

Out of fo - cus, eye to
I hear the sound of my own

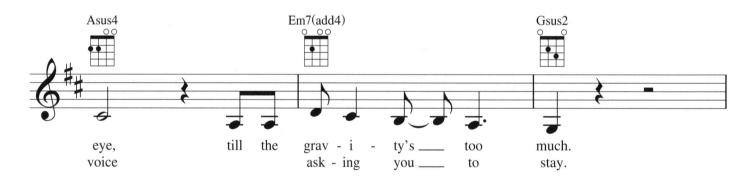

eye, till the grav - i - ty's __ too much.
voice ask - ing you __ to stay.

And I'll do an - y - thing you say, if you say it with __ your hands. __
And all we are is skin and bone, trained to get __ a - long. __

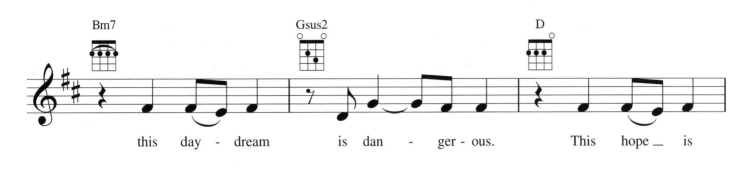

this day - dream   is dan - ger - ous.   This hope __ is

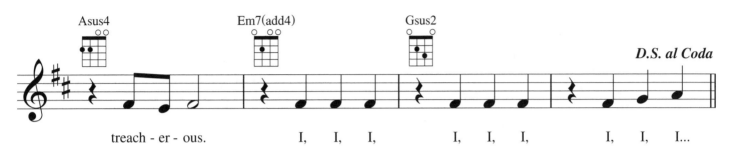

D.S. al Coda

treach - er - ous.   I, I, I,   I, I, I,   I, I, I...

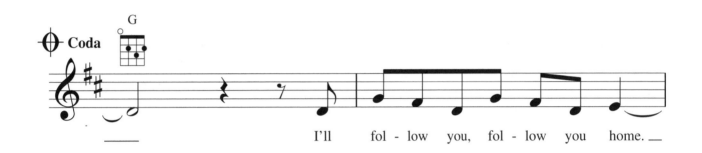

Coda

__   I'll fol - low you, fol - low you home. __

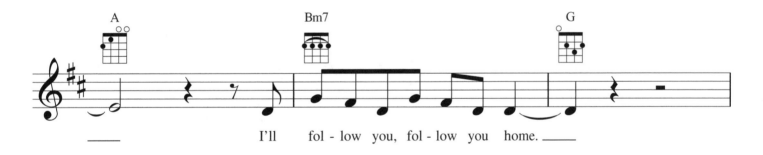

__   I'll fol - low you, fol - low you home. ____

Outro

This slope __ is ____ treach - er - ous.

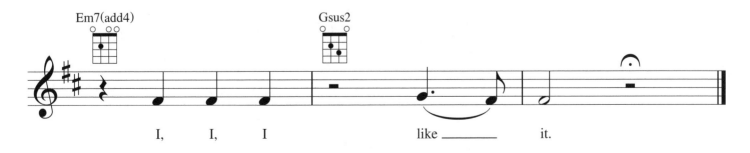

I, I, I   like ____ it.

I Knew You Were Trouble

Words and Music by Taylor Swift, Shellback and Max Martin

22

Words and Music by Taylor Swift, Shellback and Max Martin

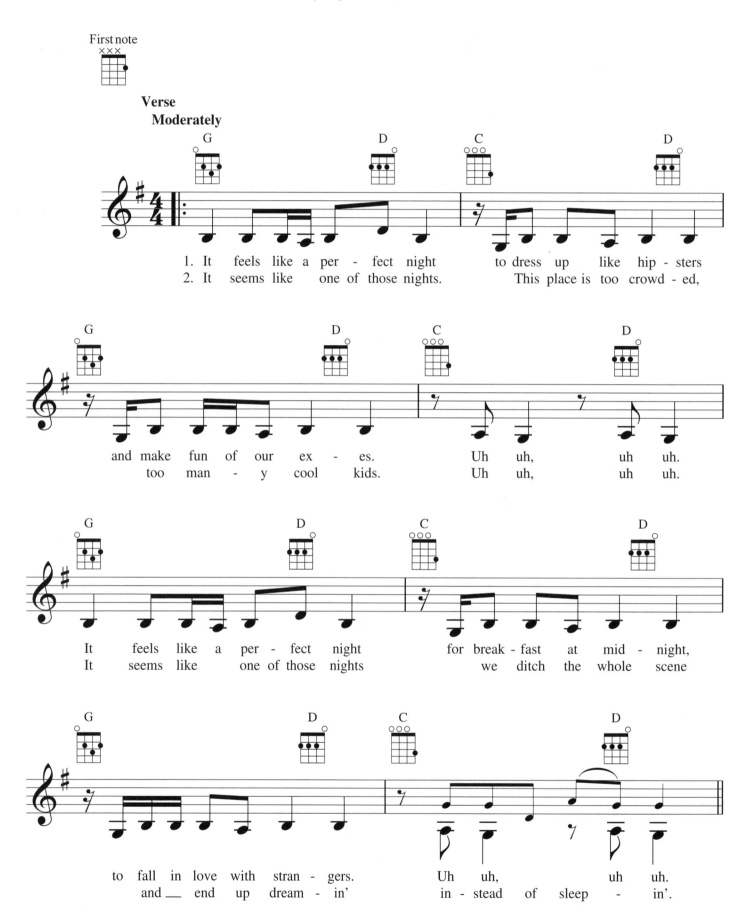

but I'll bet you want ___ to. ___ Ev-'ry-thing will be al-right if

we just keep danc-in' like we're twen-ty-two, _____

1.
twen-ty-two. _____

2., 3.
_____ Twen-ty-two, ____

_____ twen-ty-two. ____

Bridge
_____ It feels like one of those nights

32

I Almost Do

Words and Music by Taylor Swift

2. I bet you think I ei - ther moved on or hate ___

___ you, 'cause each time you ___ reach out, ___

___ there's no ___ re - ply. ___

I bet it nev - er ev - er oc - curred to you ___ that

I can't say ____ hel - lo ____ to you and risk an -

D.S. al Coda 1

oth - er good - bye. ____

Coda 1

al - most do, ____ I al - most do. ____

Interlude

Bridge

Oh, ____ we made quite a mess, ____ babe. It's

Outro-Verse

I bet this time of night you're still ___

___ up. I bet you're tired from a long, hard ___

week. ___ I bet you're

sit - tin' in your chair by the win - dow, look - in' out at the cit - y. And I ___

___ hope some - times you won - der 'bout me.

We Are Never Ever Getting Back Together

Words and Music by Taylor Swift, Shellback and Max Martin

Verse
Moderately

1. I re-mem-ber when we broke __ up the first time,

say-in', "This is it; I've had e - nough." Be - cause, like, we

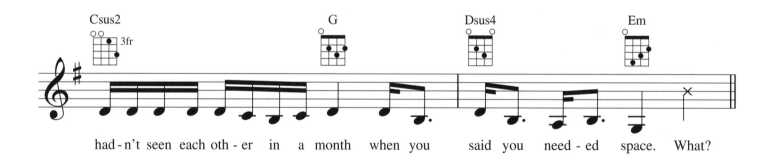

had-n't seen each oth-er in a month when you said you need-ed space. What?

Verse

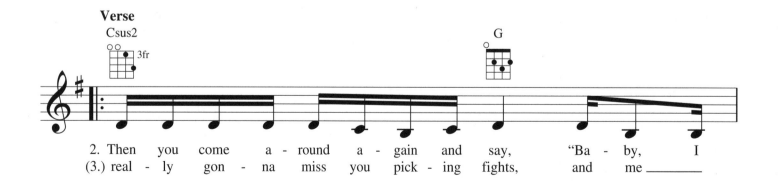

2. Then you come a-round a-gain and say, "Ba-by, I
(3.) real - ly gon-na miss you pick-ing fights, and me ___

miss you and I swear I'm gon - na change. Trust me." Re -
fall - ing for it, scream - ing that I'm right. And you would

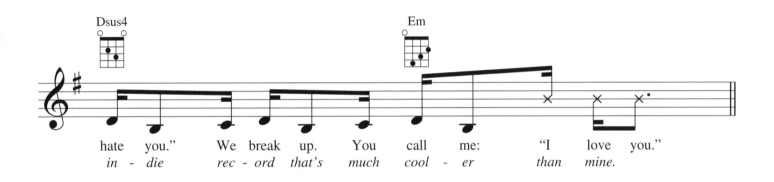

mem - ber how that last - ed for a day? I say, "I
hide a - way and find your peace of mind with some _____ *(Spoken:)*

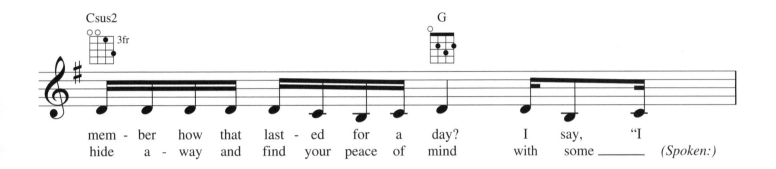

hate you." We break up. You call me: "I love you."
in - die rec - ord that's much cool - er than mine.

Pre-Chorus

Ooh, _____ ooh, ooh, ___ we called it off a - gain ___ last night. ___ But
Ooh, _____ ooh, ooh, ___ you called me up a - gain ___ to - night. ___ But

ooh, _____ ooh, ooh, ___ this time ___ I'm tell - ing you, I'm tell - ing you,
ooh, _____ ooh, ooh, ___ this time ___ I'm tell - ing you, I'm tell - ing you,

we are nev - er ev - er ev - er _____ get - ting back to - geth - er.

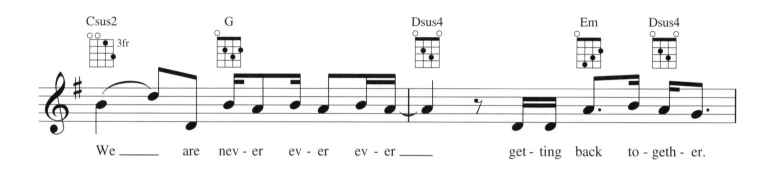

We _____ are nev - er ev - er ev - er _____ get - ting back to - geth - er.

You go talk to your __ friends, talk to my _____ friends, talk to me. __ But

To Coda ⊕

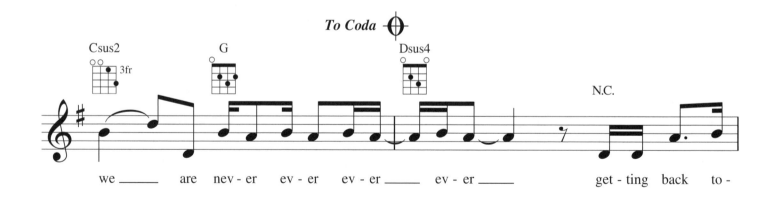

we _____ are nev - er ev - er ev - er _____ ev - er _____ get - ting back to -

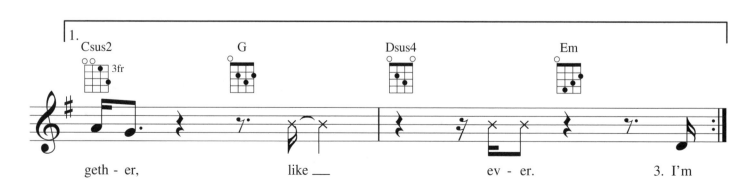

geth - er, like __ ev - er. 3. I'm

42

geth - er. ____ Ooh, ____ ooh, ooh. ___ Ooh, _____ ooh, ooh, ___ ooh,

ooh, _____ ooh, ooh. ___ Oh, oh, oh. _____

Bridge

I used to think ___ that we ____ were for - ev - er, ev - er, and

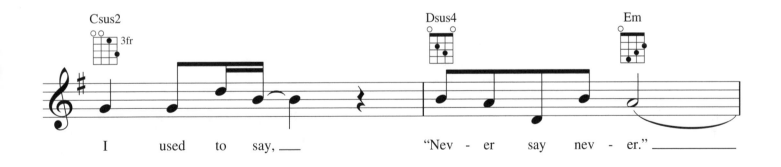

I used to say, ___ "Nev - er say nev - er." _____

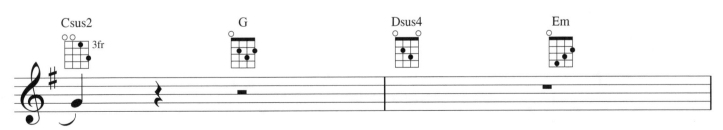

___ *(Spoken:)* *So he calls me up and he's like, "I still love you," and I'm like... I'm just... I mean,*

this is exhausting, you know? Like, we are never getting back together, like, ev - er. No,

Coda　　　　　　　　　　　　　　　　　　　　**Outro**

___ ev - er ___ get - ting back... We, ooh, ___ ooh, ooh, ___

ooh, get - ting back to - geth - er. We, ___ ooh, ___ ooh, ooh, ___

oh, ___ get - ting back to - geth - er. You go talk to your ___ friends, talk to my ___

___ friends, talk to me. ___ But we ___ are nev - er ev - er ev - er ___

___ ev - er ___ get - ting back to - geth - er.

Stay Stay Stay

Words and Music by Taylor Swift

I read you should nev-er leave a fight un-re-solved. ___
took all of their prob-lems out on me. But

That's when you came in wear-ing a foot-ball hel-met ___ and said,
you car-ry my gro-c'ries and now I'm al-ways laugh-ing. ___ I

"O - kay, let's talk." And I said:
love you be-cause you have giv-en me no choice but to

Chorus

Stay, } stay, stay. I've been lov-ing you ___ for quite ___ some
stay, }

time, time, time. You think that it's fun-ny when ___ I'm

mad, mad, mad. But I think that it's best ___ if we ___ both

stay.

Interlude

stay,   stay,   stay." __   *(Instrumental)*

Bridge

You   took   the   time   to   mem -

- o - rize   me,   my   fears,   my   hopes   and   dreams. __   I   just   like   hang - ing

out   with   you   all   the   time. _____

Chorus

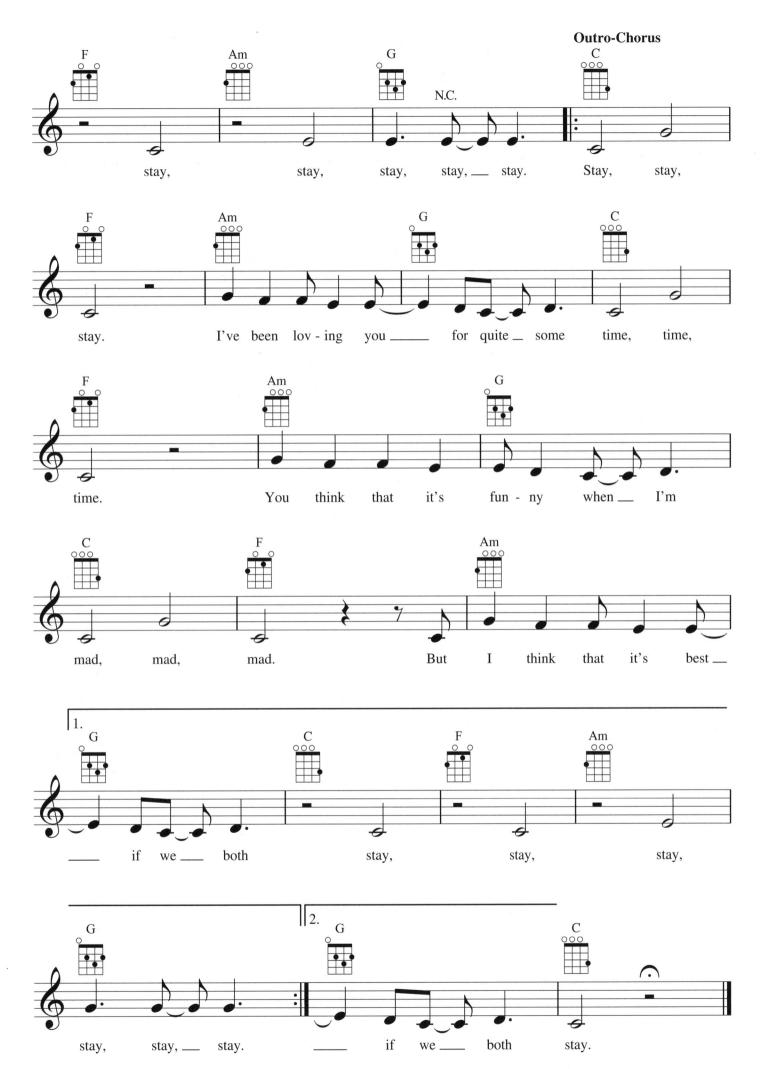

The Last Time

Words and Music by Taylor Swift, Garret Lee (Jacknife Lee) and Gary Lightbody

past,   no   rea - sons   why,   just   you   and   me.

𝄋 Chorus

This   is   the

last   time   I'm ask - ing   you   this.   Put   my   name   at   the   top   of   your   list.

This   is   the   last   time   I'm ask - ing   you   why   you   break   my

To Coda ⊕

Female:

heart   in   the   blink   of   an   eye,   eye,   eye.   2. You

Verse

find   your - self   at   my   door,   just   like   all   those   times   be - fore.   You

wear your best a-pol - o-gy, but I was there to watch __ you leave. __ And

all the times __ I let you in, ___ just for you __ to go __ a - gain, __

dis-ap-pear __ when you come back, __ ev-'ry-thing is bet-ter. And right __

Female:

Male:

Pre-Chorus

___ be - fore ___ your eyes, _____ I'm ach - ing. __ No

past, no - where ___ to hide, _____ just you and ___ me. __

Chorus

This is the

last time I'm ask-ing you this. _____ Put my name at the top of your list. _

_____ This is the last time I'm ask-ing you why _____ you break my

heart in the blink of an eye, _____ eye, _____ eye. _____

Interlude

(Instrumental)

Bridge

Female: This is the last time you tell me I've got it wrong. *Male:* This is the last time I

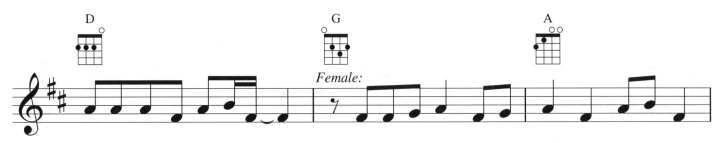

say it's been you all a - long. __ This is the last time I let you in my door.

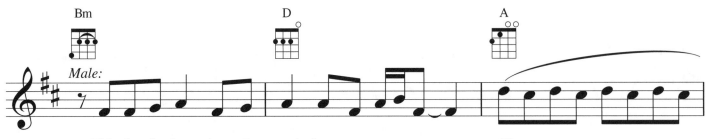

Male: This is the last time; I won't hurt you an - y - more. __ Oh. _____

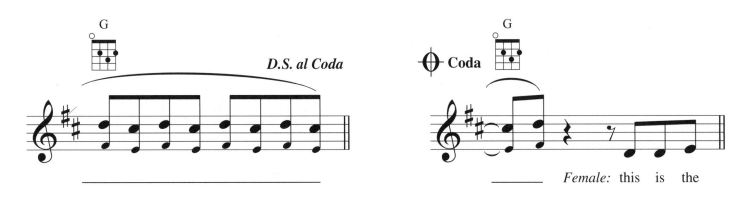

D.S. al Coda

Coda

_____ *Female:* this is the

Chorus

Male: This is the last time I'm ask - ing you this. __

last time I'm ask - ing you this. _____ Put my

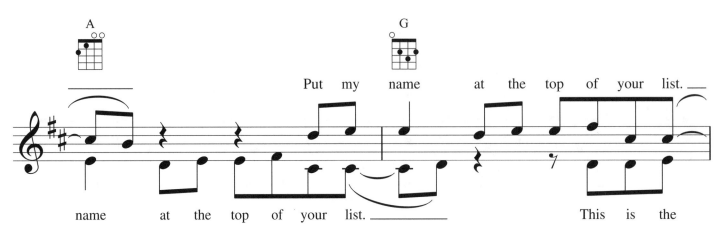

Put my name at the top of your list. __

name at the top of your list. _____ This is the

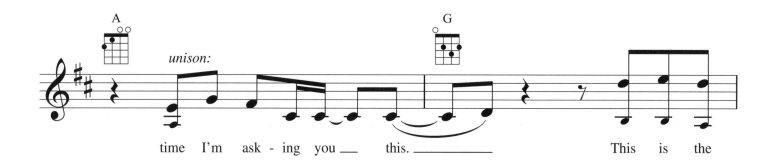

unison:
time I'm ask - ing you ___ this. _____ This is the

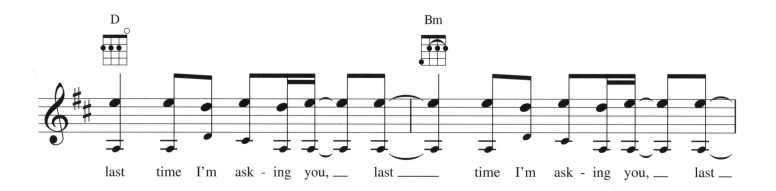

last time I'm ask - ing you, ___ last _____ time I'm ask - ing you, ___ last ___

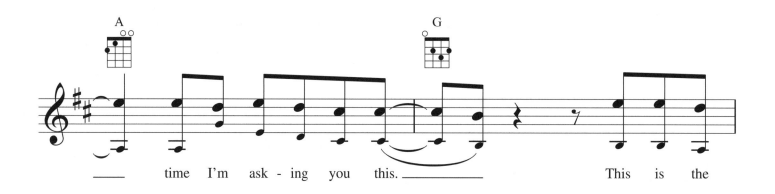

___ time I'm ask - ing you this. _____ This is the

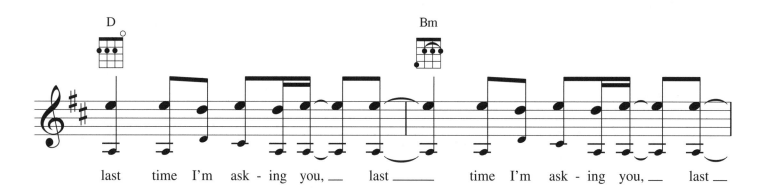

last time I'm ask - ing you, ___ last _____ time I'm ask - ing you, ___ last ___

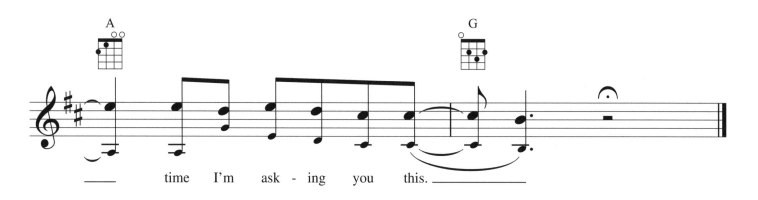

___ time I'm ask - ing you this. _____

Everything Has Changed

Words and Music by Taylor Swift and Ed Sheeran

Pre-Chorus

me feel _____ right. I just wan - na know you bet - ter, know

you bet - ter, know you bet - ter now. I just wan - na

know you bet - ter, know you bet - ter, know you bet - ter now. ___

Male: *Female:* I just wan - na know you bet - ter, know you bet - ter, know

you bet - ter now. I just wan - na know you, know ___

Chorus

Male: *Female:* ___ you, know ___ you. 'Cause all I know is we

said hel - lo ____ and your eyes look like com - in' home. _ All

I know is a sim - ple name. _____ Ev - 'ry - thing

has changed. All I know is you held the door. _

You'll be mine and I'll be yours. _ All I know since

yes - ter - day _____ is ev - 'ry - thing has changed.

Male:

2. And

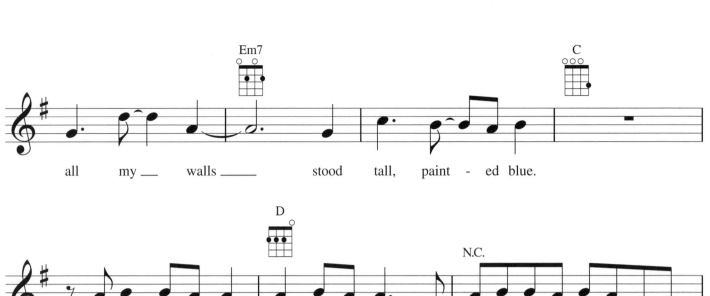

all my __ walls _____ stood tall, paint - ed blue.

But I'll take 'em down, ____ take 'em down and o - pen up the door _ for you. _

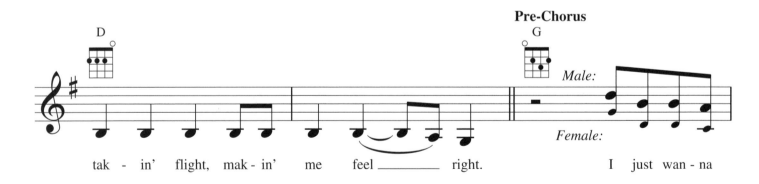

____ And all I _____ feel _____ in my

stom - ach is but - ter - flies, _____ the beau - ti - ful kind. Mak - in' up for lost time,

Pre-Chorus

tak - in' flight, mak - in' me feel _____ right.   *Male:*   I just wan - na

Female:

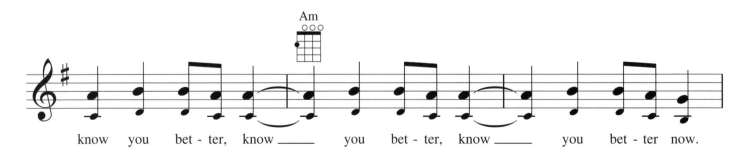

know you bet - ter, know _____ you bet - ter, know _____ you bet - ter now.

D.S. al Coda 1

Coda 1

Bridge

this time.

And meet me there to - night. And

let me know that it's not all in my

Pre-Chorus

Female:

mind. I just wan - na

know you bet - ter, know you bet - ter, know you bet - ter now.

I just wan - na know you, know you, know

Holy Ground

Words and Music by Taylor Swift

Verse
Driving

1. I was rem - in - isc - ing just the oth - er day while hav - ing

2. *See additional lyrics*

cof - fee all a - lone, and lord, it took me a - way, back to a first - glance feel - ing on

New York time, __ back when you fit my po - ems like a per - fect rhyme. ____

Took off fast - er than a green - light go. Yeah, you skip the con - ver - sa - tion when you

al - read - y know. I left a note on the door with a joke we'd made, __ and

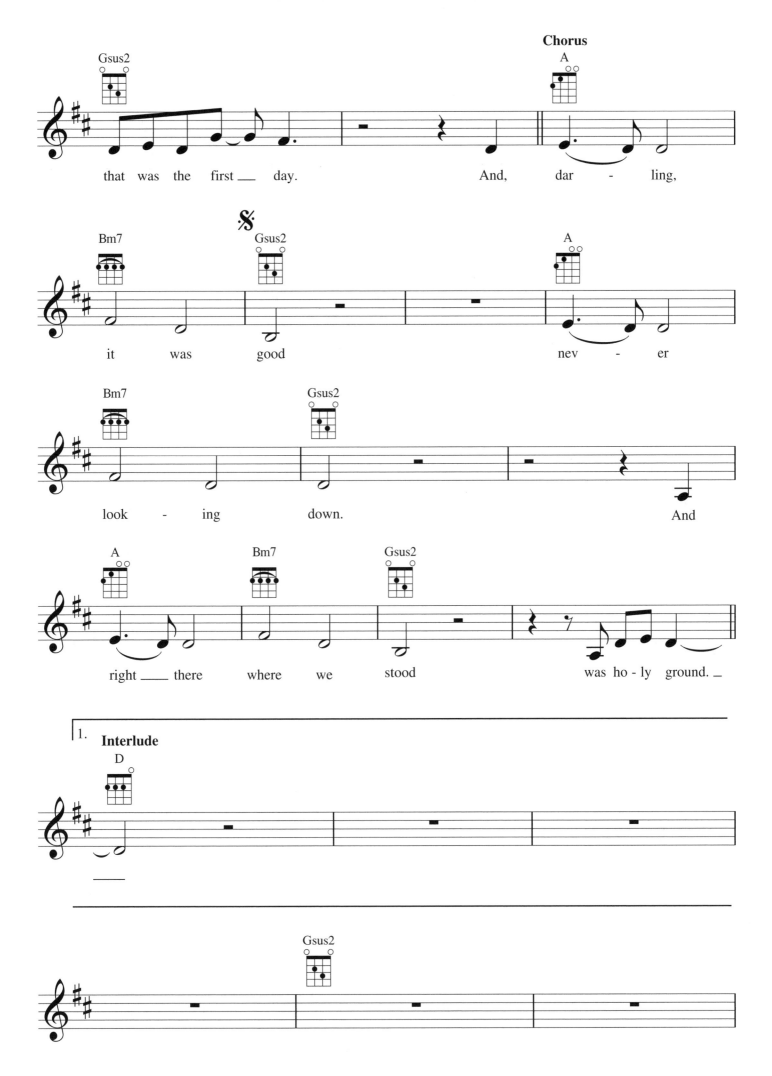

(Ooh - lay, _____ ooh - lay, _____ ooh - lay, _____ oh. _____

Ooh - lay, _____ ooh - lay, _____ ooh - lay _____

Bridge

oh.) _____ To - night I'm gon - na dance

for all that we've been through. ___ But I don't

wan - na dance if I'm not danc - ing with you.

Additional Lyrics

2. Spinning like a girl in a brand-new dress,
   We had this big wide city all to ourselves.
   We blocked the noise with the sound of "I need you,"
   And for the first time, I had something to lose.
   And I guess we fell apart in the usual way,
   And the story's got dust on every page.
   But sometimes I wonder how you think about it now,
   And I see your face in every crowd.
   'Cause... *(To Chorus)*

Sad Beautiful Tragic

Words and Music by Taylor Swift

* Sung an octave lower throughout.

- et. ____   Good __

girls,   hope - ful they'll _ be _____   and long they will __

____ wait. _____   We __

𝄋 Chorus

had   a beau - ti - ful, ___ mag - ic _____

love ____ there. _   What a

sad,   beau - ti - ful, ___ trag - ic ____

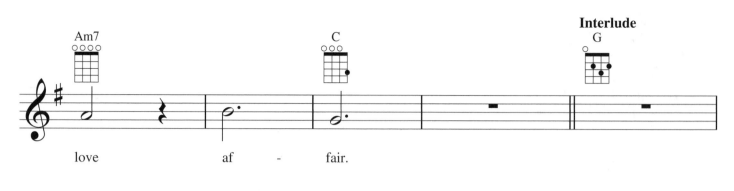

love   af -   fair.

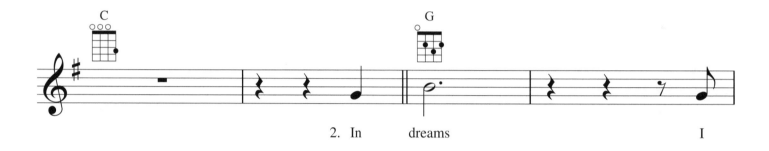

2. In   dreams   I

meet   you   in   warm ___   con - ver - sa -   tion. ___

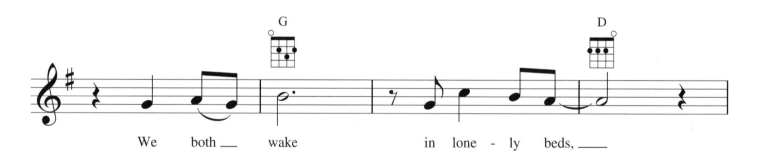

We   both ___   wake   in   lone - ly   beds, ___

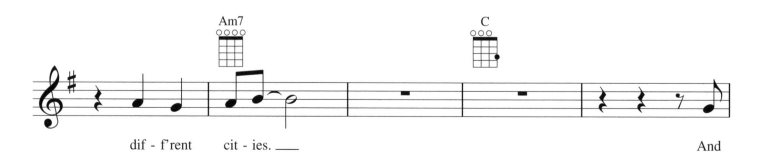

dif - f'rent   cit - ies. ___   And

70

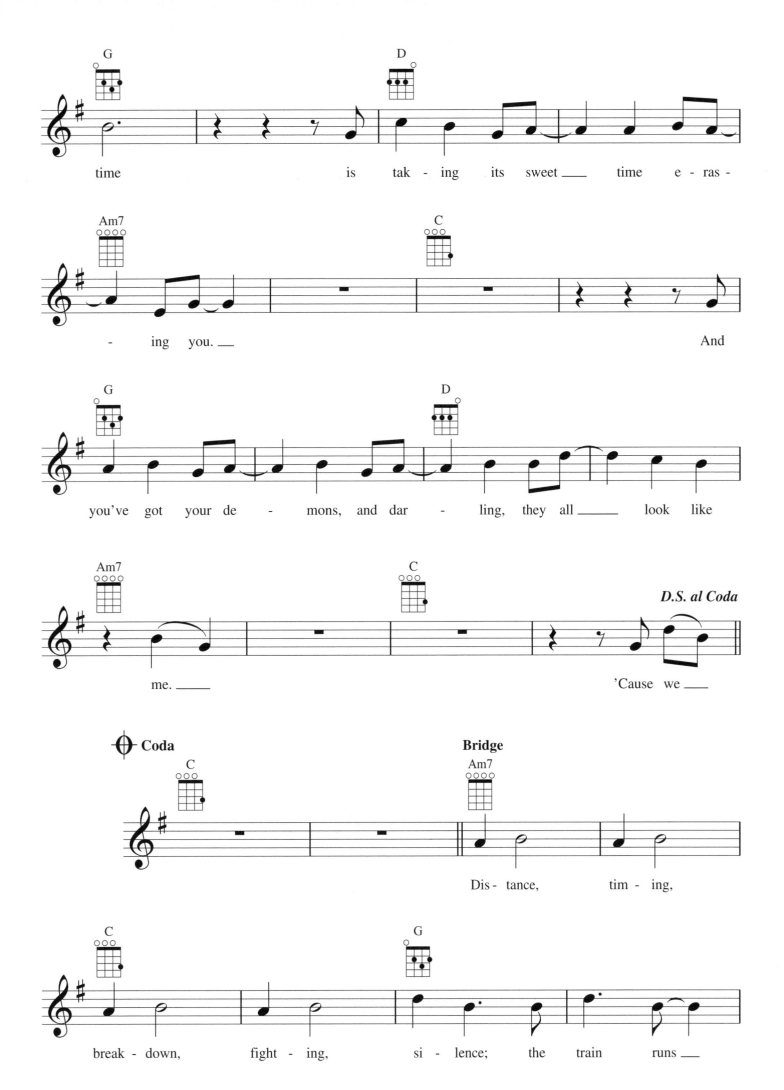

off its ____ tracks. Kiss me, try to fix it. Could

you just try to lis - ten? Hang up, give up; for the ___

life of ____ us, we ____ can't get ____ back.

Interlude-Chorus

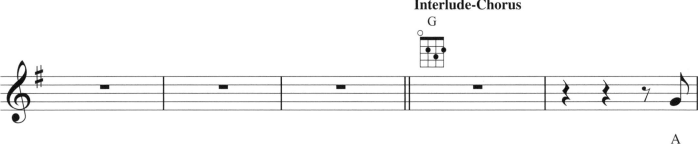

A

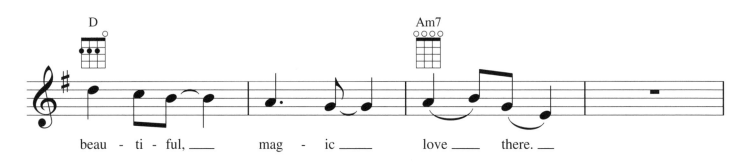

beau - ti - ful, ____ mag - ic ____ love ____ there. ___

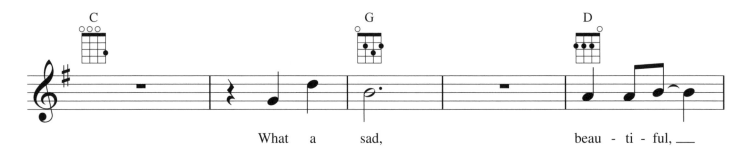

What a sad, beau - ti - ful, ___

trag - ic, ___ beau - ti - ful, ___ trag - ic, ___ beau - ti - ful... ___

Chorus

What we had, a beau - ti - ful, ___

mag - ic ___ love ___ there. ___

What a sad, beau - ti - ful, ___

trag - ic ___ love af - fair.

We ___ fair.

The Lucky One

Words and Music by Taylor Swift

First note

Verse
Moderately

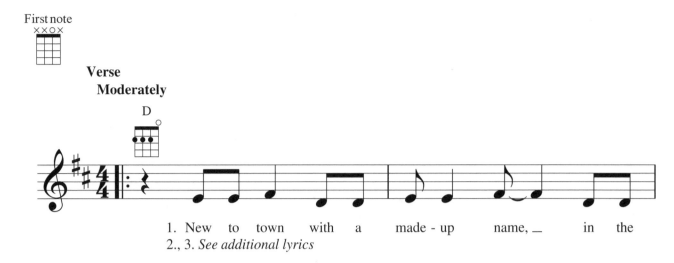

1. New to town with a made - up name, __ in the
2., 3. *See additional lyrics*

an - gels' cit - y chas - ing for - tune and fame. __ And the cam - 'ra flash - es,

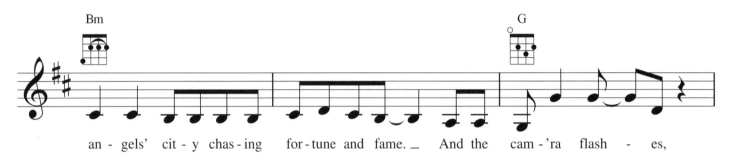

make it look __ like a dream. __

You had it fig - ured out __ since you were in __ school. __ Ev - 'ry -

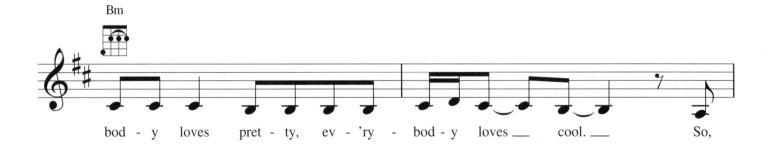

bod - y loves pret - ty, ev - 'ry - bod - y loves __ cool. __ So,

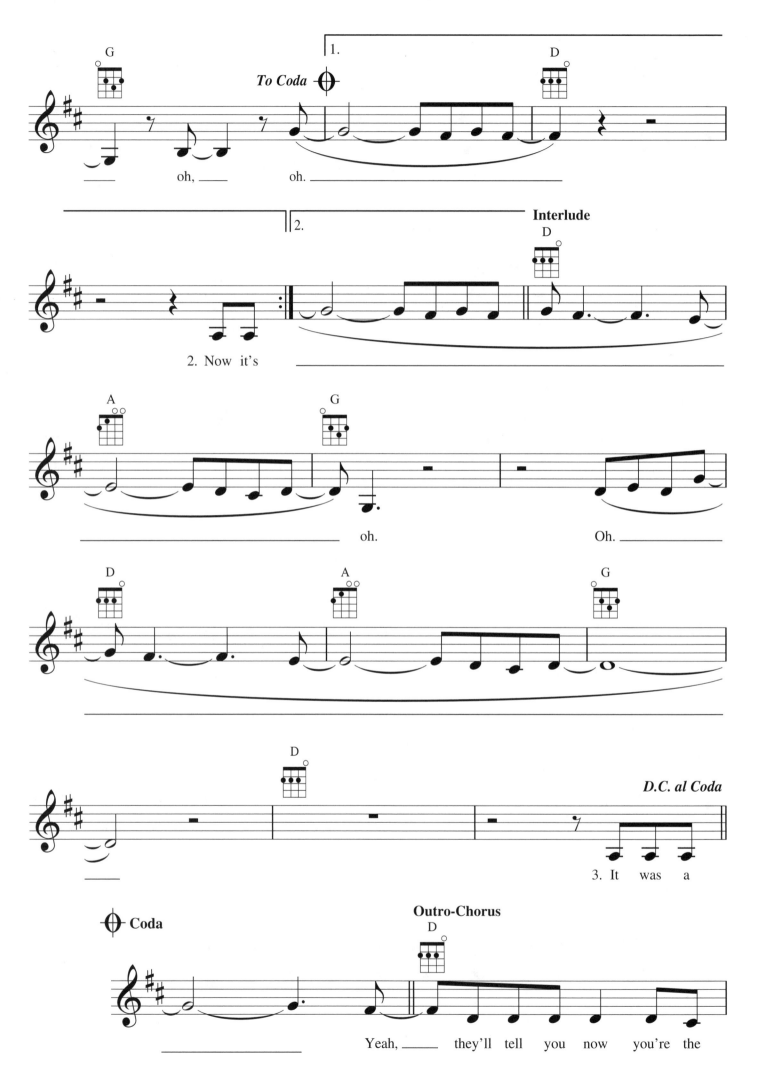

luck - y _____ one. _____ Yeah, _____ they'll tell you now you're the

luck - y _____ one. _____ Let _____ me tell you now: you're the

luck - y _____ one. _____ Oh, _____ oh, _____ oh, _____

_____ oh, oh, _____ oh.

Additional Lyrics

2. Now it's big black cars and Riviera views,
   And your lover in the foyer doesn't even know you.
   And your secrets end up splashed on the news' front page.
   And they tell you that you're lucky, but you're so confused,
   'Cause you don't feel pretty; you just feel used.
   And all the young things line up to take your place.
   Another name goes up in lights.
   You wonder if you'll make it out alive.

3. It was a few years later I showed up here,
   And they still tell the legend of how you disappeared,
   How you took the money and your dignity and got the hell out.
   They say you bought a bunch of land somewhere,
   Chose the rose garden over Madison Square.
   And it took some time, but I understand it now,
   'Cause now my name is up in lights.
   But I think you got it right.

Starlight

Words and Music by Taylor Swift

board - walk, sum - mer of for - ty - five. _____

Picked me up late one night, out the win - dow. We were sev - en-teen and cra - zy, run-

ning wild, ____ wild. Can't re - mem-ber what song it was play - ing when we

walked in, the night we snuck in - to a yacht ___ club par -

- ty, pre-tend-ing to be ____ a duch-ess and a prince. ____ And I said,

𝄋 Chorus

"Oh my, what a mar-vel-ous tune!" ___ It was the best night. Nev - er would for-

get how he moved. __ The whole place ____ was dressed to the nines __ and we were

danc - ing, danc - ing like ___ we're made of star - light, star - light,

To Coda 1
To Coda 2

like ___ we're made of star - light, star - light. _____

Verse

2. He said, "Look at you,

wor - ry - ing too much a - bout things you can't change. _____

You'll spend your whole life sing - ing the blues ___ if you keep

81

have ten kids ___ and teach 'em how to dream. _____

Coda 2

D.S. al Coda 2

_____

Like ___ we're made of

Outro

star - light, star - light, like ___ we dream im - pos - si - ble ___ dreams. ___

Like star - light, star - light, like ___ we dream im -

pos - si - ble dreams. _____ Don't ___ you see the star - light, star - light?

Don't ___ you dream im - pos - si - ble things? ___

Begin Again

Words and Music by Taylor Swift

2. Walked   in   ex - pect - ing
3. You said you nev - er   met __

you'd   be   late,   but   you   got   here   ear - ly   and   you   stand   and   wave.   I
one   girl   who   had   as   man - y   James   Tay   -   lor __   rec - ords   as   you,   but

walk   to _____ you.
I _____ do.

You   pull   my   chair   out   and   help   me   in,
We   tell __   sto - ries,   and   you   don't   know   why

and   you   don't   know   how   nice   that   is,   but   I _____ do.
I'm   com - ing   off   a   lit - tle   shy,   but   I _____ do.

I watched it be-gin a-gain. *(Instrumental)*

(Instrumental)

And we walked down the block to my car,

and I al-most brought him up, but you start to talk

HAL•LEONARD UKULELE PLAY-ALONG

Now you can play your favorite songs on your uke with great-sounding backing tracks to help you sound like a bona fide pro!

1. POP HITS
American Pie • Copacabana (At the Copa) • Crocodile Rock • Kokomo • Lean on Me • Stand by Me • Twist and Shout • What the World Needs Now Is Love.
00701451 Book/CD Pack.........................$14.99

2. UKE CLASSICS
Ain't She Sweet • Five Foot Two, Eyes of Blue (Has Anybody Seen My Girl?) • It's Only a Paper Moon • Living in the Sunlight, Loving in the Moonlight • Pennies from Heaven • Tonight You Belong to Me • Ukulele Lady • When I'm Cleaning Windows.
00701452 Book/CD Pack.........................$12.99

3. HAWAIIAN FAVORITES
Aloha Oe • Blue Hawaii • HarborLights • The Hawaiian Wedding Song (Ke Kali Nei Au) • Mele Kalikimaka • Sleepy Lagoon • Sweet Someone • Tiny Bubbles.
00701453 Book/CD Pack.........................$12.99

4. CHILDREN'S SONGS
Do-Re-Mi • The Hokey Pokey • It's a Small World • My Favorite Things • Puff the Magic Dragon • Sesame Street Theme • Splish Splash • This Land Is Your Land.
00701454 Book/CD Pack.........................$12.99

5. CHRISTMAS SONGS
Do You Hear What I Hear • Feliz Navidad • Frosty the Snow Man • Here Comes Santa Claus (Right down Santa Claus Lane) • Jingle-Bell Rock • Nuttin' for Christmas • Rudolph the Red-Nosed Reindeer • Santa Claus Is Comin' to Town.
00701696 Book/CD Pack.........................$12.99

6. LENNON & McCARTNEY
And I Love Her • Day Tripper • Here, There and Everywhere • Hey Jude • Let It Be • Norwegian Wood (This Bird Has Flown) • Nowhere Man • Yesterday.
00701723 Book/CD Pack.........................$12.99

7. DISNEY FAVORITES
Alice in Wonderland • The Bare Necessities • Candle on the Water • Chim Chim Cher-ee • A Dream Is a Wish Your Heart Makes • Mickey Mouse March • Supercalifragilisticexpialidocious • Under the Sea.
00701724 Book/CD Pack.........................$12.99

8. CHART HITS
All the Right Moves • Bubbly • Hey, Soul Sister • I'm Yours • Toes • Use Somebody • Viva la Vida • You're Beautiful.
00701745 Book/CD Pack.........................$14.99

9. THE SOUND OF MUSIC
Climb Ev'ry Mountain • Do-Re-Mi • Edelweiss • Maria • My Favorite Things • Sixteen Going on Seventeen • Something Good • The Sound of Music.
00701784 Book/CD Pack.........................$12.99

10. MOTOWN
Baby Love • Easy • How Sweet It Is (To Be Loved by You) • I Heard It Through the Grapevine • I Want You Back • My Cherie Amour • My Girl • You Can't Hurry Love.
00701964 Book/CD Pack.........................$12.99

11. CHRISTMAS STRUMMING
Away in a Manger • Deck the Hall • The First Noel • Hark! the Herald Angels Sing • Jingle Bells • Joy to the World • O Come, All Ye Faithful (Adeste Fideles) • We Three Kings of Orient Are.
00702458 Book/CD Pack.........................$12.99

12. BLUEGRASS FAVORITES
Angel Band • Dooley • Fox on the Run • I Am a Man of Constant Sorrow • I'll Fly Away • Keep on the Sunny Side • Sitting on Top of the World • With Body and Soul.
00702584 Book/CD Pack.........................$12.99

13. UKULELE SONGS
Daughter • Dream a Little Dream of Me • Elderly Woman Behind the Counter in a Small Town • Last Kiss • More ThanYou Know • Sleepless Nights • Tonight You Belong to Me • Yellow Ledbetter.
00702599 Book/CD Pack.........................$12.99

14. JOHNNY CASH
Cry, Cry, Cry • Daddy Sang Bass • Folsom Prison Blues • Hey, Porter • I Walk the Line • Jackson • (Ghost) Riders in the Sky (A Cowboy Legend) • Ring of Fire.
00702615 Book/CD Pack.........................$14.99

15. COUNTRY CLASSICS
Achy Breaky Heart (Don't Tell My Heart) • Chattahoochee • Crazy • King of the Road • Rocky Top • Tennessee Waltz • You Are My Sunshine • Your Cheatin' Heart.
00702834 Book/CD Pack.........................$12.99

16. STANDARDS
Ain't Misbehavin' • All of Me • Beyond the Sea • Georgia on My Mind • Mister Sandman • Moon River • That's Amoré (That's Love) • Unchained Melody.
00702835 Book/CD Pack.........................$12.99

17. POP STANDARDS
Every Breath You Take • Fields of Gold • I Just Called to Say I Love You • Kansas City • Killing Me Softly with His Song • Sunny • Tears in Heaven • What a Wonderful World.
00702836 Book/CD Pack.........................$12.99

23. TAYLOR SWIFT
Crazier • Fearless • Love Story • Mean • Our Song • Teardrops on My Guitar • White Horse • You Belong with Me.
00704106 Book/CD Pack.........................$14.99

24. WINTER WONDERLAND
All I Want for Christmas Is My Two Front Teeth • Blue Christmas • The Christmas Song (Chestnuts Roasting on an Open Fire) • Have Yourself a Merry Little Christmas • Let It Snow! Let It Snow! Let It Snow! • Little Saint Nick • Sleigh Ride • Winter Wonderland.
00101871 Book/CD Pack.........................$12.99

HAL•LEONARD® CORPORATION
7777 W. BLUEMOUND RD. P.O. BOX 13819 MILWAUKEE, WI 53213

www.halleonard.com

Prices, contents, and availability subject to change without notice.

0912